KINGFISHER
READERS

level
1

Tyrannosaurus!

Thea Feldman

First published 2014 by Kingfisher
an imprint of Macmillan Children's Books
a division of Macmillan Publishers Limited
20 New Wharf Road, London N1 9RR
Basingstoke and Oxford
Associated companies throughout the world
www.panmacmillan.com

Series editor: Polly Goodman
Literacy consultant: Ellie Costa, Bank Street School for Children, New York
UK literacy consultant: Hilary Horton
Dinosaur consultant: David Burnie
Illustrations by: Sebastian Quigley, Linden Artists

ISBN: 978-0-7534-3664-6
Copyright © Macmillan Publishers Ltd 2014

9 8 7 6 5 4 3 2 1
1TR/0913/WKT/UG/105MA

A CIP catalogue record for this book is available from the British Library.

Printed in China

Picture credits
The Publisher would like to thank the following for permission to reproduce their
material. Every care has been taken to trace copyright holders. However, if there have
been unintentional omissions or failure to trace copyright holders, we apologize and
will, if informed, endeavour to make corrections in any future edition.
Top = t; Bottom = b; Centre = c; Left = l; Right = r
Pages 10t Shutterstock/Computer Earth; 10b Shutterstock/Karel Gallas; 11t Shutterstock/
Bull's-Eye Arts; 11b Shutterstock/Heiko Kiera; 28 Science Photo Library/John Mitchell;
29 Shutterstock/joingate; 30–31 Alamy/© David R. Frazier Photolibrary, Inc.

This is a big, fierce **dinosaur**!

It is called Tyrannosaurus
(Tie-RAN-oh-SAW-russ).

Tyrannosaurus lived
millions of years ago.

That is a very long
time ago.

There were no people then.

Let's go back in time
and take a look at
Tyrannosaurus!

Tyrannosaurus is hungry!

He is looking for food.

What does he eat?

Other dinosaurs!
Tyrannosaurus is a hunter.

The animals he hunts
are called his **prey**.

Triceratops (Try-SER-uh-tops) might become his prey.

So might Edmontosaurus (Ed-MON-toe-SORE-us).

Here are some
other animals
that live in the
same forest.

Tyrannosaurus does
not eat them.

Tyrannosaurus is big.

He needs a lot of food.

So he hunts big animals.

Look!

Tyrannosaurus runs after his prey.

He runs on his toes.

His tail sticks out behind him.

The tail helps Tyrannosaurus keep his balance.

Tyrannosaurus catches up with his prey.

He tries to bite Triceratops.

Triceratops fights back with her sharp horns.

Triceratops gets away!

Tyrannosaurus is still hungry.

He runs
through the
forest again.

Tyrannosaurus meets
another Tyrannosaurus.

The two dinosaurs fight.

Why?

Maybe they do not want
to share the same part
of the forest.

One Tyrannosaurus
sinks his teeth
into the other.

The other Tyrannosaurus
runs away.

The winner smells
something new
in the air.

What is it?

It is an Edmontosaurus
that has died.

Tyrannosaurus gulps down
200 kilograms of meat in
one bite!

Tyrannosaurus had a busy day.

He is full and ready for a nap.

How does he sleep?

He can close his eyes
and sleep standing up!

Sometimes he lies
down on the ground.

Dinosaurs lived millions of years ago.

All the dinosaurs are now **extinct**.

This means they have all died.

How do we know so much about them?

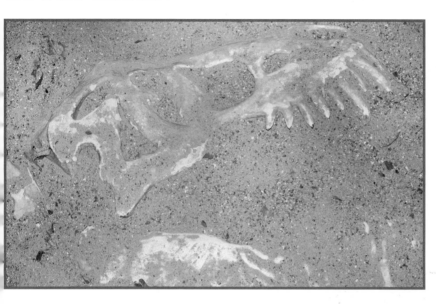

Scientists find dinosaur bones buried in the ground.

These old bones are called **fossils**.

Scientists study the fossils.

The biggest Tyrannosaurus was found in the USA.

It is named Sue after the scientist who found it.

You can tell just by looking at Sue that Tyrannosaurus was a big, fierce dinosaur!

Glossary

dinosaur a kind of animal that lived millions of years ago

extinct a kind of animal or plant that no longer exists

fossils parts of dead animals that have turned to stone

prey animals that are hunted and eaten by other animals

scientists people who study science and use it in their work

BC 03/14